A Bouquet of Promises

For:

From:

Red Rose: Jeanette Hender

Compiled by Judith Merrell

Psalm 145:13
The LORD is faithful to all his promises and loving towards
all he has made. (NIV)

Yellow rose
Judith Merrel

Needing Encouragement

Psalm 103:11-12
How great is God's love for all who worship him?
Greater than the distance between heaven and earth!
How far has the LORD taken our sins from us?
Further than the distance from east to west!
(CEV)

•

Isaiah 46:4
I will still be the same when you are old and grey,
and I will take care of you.
I created you. I will carry you
and always keep you safe.
(CEV)

Matthew 10:29-30

What's the price of a pet canary?
Some loose change, right?
And God cares what happens to it
even more than you do. He pays even
greater attention to you, down to the
last detail – even numbering the hairs
on your head! (The Message)

Matthew 18:20

For where two or three come together
in my name, there am I with them. (NIV)

John 10:10

I have come that they may have life,
and have it to the full. (NIV)

John 12:46

I am the light that has come into the
world. No one who has faith in me will
stay in the dark. (CEV)

Chrysanthemum:
Jonathan Merrell

Alstroemeria: Lucinda Harris

Romans 8:28

And we know that in all things God works for the good of those who love him, who have been called according to his purpose. (NIV)

᛫

Romans 8:31-32

With God on our side like this, how can we lose? If God didn't hesitate to put everything on the line for us, embracing our condition and exposing himself to the worst by sending his own Son, is there anything else he wouldn't gladly and freely do for us? (The Message)

᛫

Romans 8:38-39

For I am certain that nothing can separate us from his love: neither death nor life, neither angels nor other heavenly rulers or powers, neither the present nor the future, neither the world above nor the world below – there is nothing in all creation that will ever be able to separate us from the love of God which is ours through Christ Jesus our Lord. (GNB)

᛫

Hebrews 13:8

Jesus Christ never changes!
He is the same yesterday,
today, and forever. (CEV)

Rhododendron: Daniel Boddison

Needing Reassurance

Deuteronomy 7:9
Know this: God, your God,
is God indeed, a God you
can depend upon.
(The Message)

·

Matthew 28:20
I will be with you always,
even until the end
of the world.
(CEV)

God so loved the whole world...

Johannes 3:16

Also hat Gott die Welt geliebt, daß er seinen eingeborenen
Sohn gab, auf daß alle, die an ihn glauben, nicht verloren werden,
sondern das ewige Leben haben.
(Luther Bibel – German)

•

Giovanni 3:16

Perché Dio ha tanto amato il mondo da dare il suo unico Figlio,
affinché chiunque crede in lui non perisca, ma abbia vita eterna.
(La Parola è Vita – Italian)

•

Jean 3:16

Car Dieu a tant aimé le monde qu'il a donné son Fils unique, afin que
quiconque croit en lui ne périsse point, mais qu'il ait la vie éternelle.
(Louis Segond – French)

•

Juan 3:16

Porque tanto amó Dios al mundo, que dio a su Hijo unigénito, para que
todo el que cree en él no se pierda, sino que tenga vida eterna.
(Nueva Versión Internacional – Spanish)

John 3:16
For God so loved the world that he gave his one and only Son, that whoever believes in him shall not perish but have eternal life. (NIV)

Water Lilies
David McMurray

Centranthus Ruber: Jonathan Merrell

John 14:16-17

Then I will ask the Father to send you the Holy Spirit who will help you and always be with you. The Spirit will show you what is true.

(CEV)

•

2 Corinthians 5:17

Anyone who belongs to Christ is a new person. The past is forgotten, and everything is new.

(CEV)

Wild poppy

Needing
Guidance

Nigella: Mary Fisher

Proverbs 3:5-6
Trust in the LORD with all your heart and lean not on your own understanding; in all your ways acknowledge him, and he will make your paths straight. (NIV)

•

Proverbs 16:3
Commit to the LORD whatever you do, and your plans will succeed. (NIV)

•

Isaiah 30:21
Whether you turn to the right or to the left, your ears will hear a voice behind you, saying, "This is the way; walk in it." (NIV)

Isaiah 42:16
But I'll take the hand of those who don't know the way,
who can't see where they're going.
I'll be a personal guide to them,
directing them through unknown country.
I'll be right there to show them what roads to take,
make sure they don't fall into the ditch.
These are the things I'll be doing for them –
sticking with them, not leaving them for a minute.
(The Message)

•

Jeremiah 29:11
For I know the plans I have for you, declares the LORD, plans to prosper
you and not to harm you, plans to give you hope and a future. (NIV)

•

Matthew 7:7-8
Ask and it will be given to you; seek and you will find;
knock and the door will be opened to you. For everyone who asks receives;
he who seeks finds; and to him who knocks, the door will be opened.
(NIV)

James 1:5
If any of you need
wisdom, you should
ask God, and it will
be given to you.
(CEV)

Viola:
Liz Edwards

Red rose: Jeanette Hender

Needing Strength

Psalm 18:2
The Lord is my protector;
he is my strong fortress.
My God is my protection,
and with him I am safe.
He protects me like a shield;
he defends me and keeps me safe.
(GNB)

•

Psalm 28:7
The LORD is my strength and my
shield; my heart trusts in him, and I
am helped. My heart leaps for joy and
I will give thanks to him in song. (NIV)

Isaiah 40:31
But those who trust in the Lord for help
will find their strength renewed.
They will rise on wings like eagles;
they will run and not get weary;
they will walk and not grow weak.
(GNB)

Helenium: Mary Fisher

John 6:35
Then Jesus declared, "I am the bread of life.
He who comes to me will never go hungry,
and he who believes in me will never be thirsty." (NIV)

•

Revelation 21:6
I am the Alpha and the Omega, the Beginning
and the End. To him who is thirsty I will give to drink
without cost from the spring of the
water of life. (NIV)

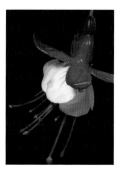

Fuschia: David McMurray

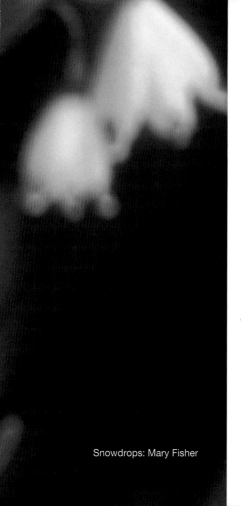

Needing Courage

Deuteronomy 33:27
The eternal God is your
refuge, and underneath
are the everlasting arms.
(NIV)

Snowdrops: Mary Fisher

Joshua 1:5

As I was with Moses,
so I will be with you;
I will never leave you
nor forsake you. (NIV)

•

Joshua 1:9

Have I not commanded you?
Be strong and courageous.
Do not be terrified;
do not be discouraged,
for the LORD your God will be with you
wherever you go. (NIV)

•

Psalm 91:11

God will command his angels to protect
you wherever you go. (CEV)

Spring in Kent:
David McMurray

Hebrews 13:5
The Lord has promised that he will not leave us or desert us. (CEV)

Michaelmas daisy: Carolyn Lewis

Needing Peace

Psalm 4:8
I can lie down and sleep soundly
because you, LORD, will keep me safe.
(CEV)

•

Psalm 23:2-3
You let me rest in fields of green grass.
You lead me to streams of peaceful water,
and you refresh my life. (CEV)

•

Psalm 29:11
The LORD gives strength to his people
and blesses them with peace. (GNB)

John 14:27
I give you peace,
the kind of peace that only I can give.
It isn't like the peace
that this world can give.
So don't be worried or afraid. (CEV)

•

Philippians 4:6-7
Do not be anxious about anything, but in everything, by prayer and petition, with thanksgiving, present your requests to God. And the peace of God, which transcends all understanding, will guard your hearts and your minds in Christ Jesus. (NIV)

•

2 Thessalonians 3:16
I pray that the Lord, who gives peace, will always bless you with peace. May the Lord be with all of you. (CEV)

Crocus: Maria Flenley

Coping with Sadness
or Bereavement

Narcissi: Judith Merrell

Psalm 34:17-18
Is anyone crying for help? God
is listening, ready to rescue you.
If your heart is broken,
you'll find God right there...
(The Message)

Primrose: Judith Merrell

Psalm 147:3-5

He heals the broken-hearted and binds up their wounds. He determines the number of the stars and calls them each by name. Great is our Lord and mighty in power; his understanding has no limit. (NIV)

•

Isaiah 25:8

He will swallow up death in victory; and the Lord GOD will wipe away tears from off all faces... (KJV)

•

Jeremiah 31:13

I will turn their mourning into gladness; I will give them comfort and joy instead of sorrow. (NIV)

Matthew 5:4
God blesses those people
who grieve. They will find
comfort! (CEV)

White rose: David McMurra

John 14:1-3

Do not let your hearts be troubled. Trust in God; trust also in me.
In my Father's house are many rooms; if it were not so, I would have told you. I am going there to prepare a place for you.
And if I go and prepare a place for you, I will come back and take you to be with me that you also may be where I am. (NIV)

•

Revelation 21:1, 3-4

I saw a new heaven and a new earth. The first heaven and the first earth had disappeared, and so had the sea...
...Yes, God will make his home among his people. He will wipe all tears from their eyes, and there will be no more death, suffering, crying, or pain. These things of the past are gone forever. (CEV)

Chrysanthemums:
Tim Sandall

Poppies: Mary Fisher

Feeling
Stressed

Psalm 46:1
God is our refuge
and strength,
an ever-present
help in trouble.
(NIV)

Psalm 55:22

Pile your troubles on God's shoulders –
he'll carry your load, he'll help you out. (The Message)

●

Isaiah 43:2

Don't be afraid, I've redeemed you.
I've called your name. You're mine.
When you're in over your head, I'll be there with you.
When you're in rough waters, you will not go down.
When you're between a rock and a hard place,
it won't be a dead end –
Because I am GOD, your personal God,
The Holy of Israel, your Saviour. (The Message)

●

Matthew 11:28

Come to me, all you who are weary and burdened,
and I will give you rest. (NIV)

Marigold: Liz Edwards

James 4:8
Come near to God
and he will
come near to you.
(NIV)

Feeling Worried

Isaiah 41:10
Don't panic. I'm with you.
There's no need to fear for I'm your God.
I'll give you strength. I'll help you.
I'll hold you steady,
keep a firm grip on you.
(The Message)

•

Nahum 1:7
The LORD is good. He protects those
who trust him in times of trouble. (CEV)

Pelargonium: Jonathan Merrell

Matthew 6:34
Give your entire attention to
what God is doing right now,
and don't get worked up about
what may or may not happen
tomorrow. God will help you
deal with whatever hard things
come up when the time comes.
(The Message)

Pink dahlia: David McMurray

Luke 12:25
Who of you by worrying can add a
single hour to his life? (NIV)

•

Romans 8:28
And we know that in all things
God works for the good of those
who love him, who have been called
according to his purpose. (NIV)

•

1 Corinthians 10:13
And God is faithful; he will not let you
be tempted beyond what you can bear.
But when you are tempted, he will
also provide a way out so that you can
stand up under it. (NIV)

•

1 Peter 5:7
God cares for you, so turn all your
worries over to him. (CEV)

Bible Index